Original title:
The Land of Shadows

Copyright © 2024 Creative Arts Management OÜ
All rights reserved.

Author: Kieran Blackwood
ISBN HARDBACK: 978-9916-88-866-7
ISBN PAPERBACK: 978-9916-88-867-4

Bittersweet Farewell to Light

In twilight's glow, we whisper soft,
The sun descends, a golden croft.
Shadows stretch, the day must part,
A bittersweet ache in every heart.

Memories dance like fading dusk,
Embers glow with warmth and trust.
Yet clouds approach, they swallow hope,
A fleeting dream, we learn to cope.

Stars emerge, a twinkling sigh,
As daylight bids its sweet goodbye.
In each goodbye, a new hello,
The cycle turns, the moon will grow.

Yet longing lingers in the air,
A tender pulse, a silent prayer.
Though light may fade, love holds tight,
In every heart, it sparks the night.

Lanterns of the Lost

In the night where shadows creep,
Lanterns flicker, secrets keep.
Whispers echo, hearts once bound,
Guiding souls through hallowed ground.

Footsteps light on ancient stone,
Memories carved, yet left alone.
Each lantern held a tale of old,
Fires burning but never told.

Dreams in the Deepening Gloom

Close your eyes and drift away,
Feel the night begin to sway.
Dreams dance softly, shadows play,
In the gloam, where wishes stay.

Stars emerge, a gentle guide,
Filling hearts where dreams abide.
In the twilight's tender grace,
Hopes awaken, time and space.

Where the Light Seems to Linger

Amidst the trees where soft winds sigh,
Light breaks through the darkened sky.
A warm embrace, a loving glow,
Where the light seems to linger so.

Paths unfold with radiant beams,
Illuminating hidden dreams.
In gentle warmth, the heart can soar,
Finding solace forevermore.

Faint Glimmers of Memory

Faint glimmers spark in faded halls,
Echoes lingering through the walls.
Each moment trapped like fireflies,
Dancing softly, time denies.

In reflections, we seek to find,
The stories woven in our minds.
Faint glimmers light the way we tread,
Carrying whispers of the dead.

Murmurs from the Abyss

In shadows deep, the whispers dwell,
Stories lost in an ancient shell.
Echoes rise from the silent night,
Tales of sorrow, veiled in fright.

Oceans roar with a ghostly song,
Calling forth what feels so wrong.
A haunting breeze that sings my name,
In the darkness, there's no shame.

Waves that crash with secrets told,
In depths where hearts once bold.
Murmurs call, but I can't see,
What lies beneath the haunting sea.

Dancers Among the Shade

In twilight's glow, they swirl and sway,
Figures lost in the dying day.
Woodland spirits, light as air,
Dancing free without a care.

Leaves will rustle, a gentle tune,
Beneath the watchful, fading moon.
Footsteps soft on the forest floor,
Whispers echo, forevermore.

Elusive forms, they flit and glide,
Among the shadows, they freely bide.
With every leap, they break the gloom,
Filling night with magic's bloom.

Fragments of a Fading Light

In the dusk, fragments drift away,
Memories bathed in the end of day.
A flicker dims in the waning sky,
Leaving traces of a whispered sigh.

Stars may twinkle, but they grow pale,
As shadows weave their somber tale.
Softly falling, the dreams take flight,
Chasing echoes beyond the night.

With every flicker, a chance to find,
Pieces of a once vibrant mind.
Hold them close, let your heart ignite,
In the beauty of fading light.

Specters of Forgotten Dreams

In corners dim, the specters creep,
Haunting visions, secrets to keep.
Whispers linger in heavy air,
Fading wishes, a silent prayer.

Echoes wander through empty halls,
Carrying tales of ancient calls.
Forgotten dreams, like dust on shelves,
Lost in the depths of shadowed selves.

Yearning souls seek the light once known,
In crumbling spaces where hope is sown.
A flicker shines through the cloak of night,
Guiding lost dreams back to the light.

Ethereal Lullabies at Sundown

The sun dips low, a fiery glow,
Whispers of breezes, soft like snow.
Colors merge in the fading light,
Dreams awaken with the coming night.

Stars twinkle gently, a soft parade,
Moonbeams dance, the shadows fade.
Crickets serenade the evening's sighs,
While quiet wishes take to the skies.

Clouds embrace the twilight grace,
Nature's canvas, an endless space.
Time slows down as the world unwinds,
In this moment, peace finds our minds.

Embrace the night with hearts set free,
Ethereal songs drift over the sea.
Each lullaby a tender embrace,
At sundown's edge, we find our place.

Sentinels of the Lingering Night

Silent sentinels in the dark,
Guardians watch o'er the sleeping park.
Gentle breezes carry whispered tales,
As the moonlight softly unveils.

The stars align in a grand ballet,
Marking a path for the dreams to sway.
Each flicker holds a secret bright,
In the watchful calm of the night.

Echoes of laughter float through the air,
Memories linger, precious and rare.
The night embraces, a velvet shroud,
As the world sleeps beneath its cloud.

In stillness dwells a magic profound,
Where hope and wonder can abound.
Sentinels stand, steadfast and true,
Guarding the dreams that are yet to ensue.

Echoes of What Was

In the quiet hour, shadows play,
Memories linger, refuse to sway.
Whispers of laughter, echoes of time,
Fading like echoes, soft as a rhyme.

Golden moments held in the heart,
Each one cherished, though we're apart.
Images painted on the canvas of night,
Flickering softly in fading light.

Stories of love, both lost and found,
Resonate gently, a haunting sound.
In the silence, we feel their trace,
Echoes of what was, timeless embrace.

Time does not steal what we hold dear,
In twilight's grasp, our hearts draw near.
As stars above begin to gleam,
We find our solace in every dream.

Revelations at the Edge of Dark

Beyond the horizon where shadows creep,
Lies a secret that silence keeps.
At the edge of dark, truths take flight,
In a gentle murmur that feels so right.

The night unfolds with a quiet grace,
Filling the void, a warm embrace.
Stars become glimpses of hopes yet bright,
Revelations bloom in the depths of night.

Every heartbeat whispers a story rare,
Carried along on the cool night air.
Illuminated by the moon's soft glow,
We seek the path that we long to know.

As darkness dances, fears drift away,
In this sacred moment, we dare to stay.
Revelations come to those who believe,
At the edge of dark, we find what we achieve.

Labors of the Spirit in the Stillness

In quiet breaths, the heart does yearn,
For whispers deep, where shadows turn.
Every pause, a chance to mend,
In silent spaces, spirits bend.

Threads of light in dusky fog,
Reveal the truth, unmask the smog.
Within us all, a song concealed,
In stillness found, our souls revealed.

Embrace the calm, the aching void,
In solitude, we are enjoyed.
With gentle hands, we forge and weave,
The tapestry of what we believe.

Through labor's grace, we seek the peak,
In hidden trails, we dare to speak.
When silence reigns, the spirit thrives,
In stillness, life's true essence lies.

The Poetry of the Veiled

Beneath the fabric, stories bloom,
In shadows cast, they find their room.
Veils of dusk, with secrets lined,
In whispered tones, our souls entwined.

Each starlit night, a verse unspooled,
In moonlit dreams, we are all schooled.
The magic spun in shadowed light,
Invokes the courage to take flight.

What hides behind each silken thread?
Mysteries dance where angels tread.
With each layer, the world unfolds,
Revealing truths that time holds.

In every silence, echoes call,
A poetry that binds us all.
Veiled in grace, the heart takes flight,
In shadows deep, we find our light.

Shadows that Weep

In twilight hours, the shadows sigh,
With liquid grief, they seem to cry.
Each tear a tale, a silent plea,
For lost tomorrows, set free.

The weight of time upon their backs,
In hushed corners, they leave tracks.
Whispers echo in the gloom,
As darkened figures softly loom.

Yet in their sorrow, strength is found,
A beauty deep, though tightly wound.
The ache of night, the dawn will break,
From shadows' hold, our spirits wake.

So heed their calls, the weeping night,
For from their tears, emerges light.
In every drop, a story sleeps,
In shadows soft, the heart still weeps.

Chronicles of the Unseen

Beneath the surface, stories lie,
In hidden realms, where dreams can fly.
Chronicles penned in ink of stars,
A tapestry of cosmic scars.

What's lost in sight, still breathes and beats,
In silent halls, where fate retreats.
Through forgotten paths, our spirits roam,
In every heart, we find our home.

The unseen hands that guide our way,
Retrace the steps of yesterday.
In whispered winds, the past will speak,
In every echo, truths we seek.

So listen close, the tales unfold,
In shadows cast, and legends told.
A journey vast, though rarely seen,
Awakens souls in realms between.

Whispers of a Dim Horizon

The sky wears a coat of grey,
Soft whispers seek to sway.
In valleys low, the shadows creep,
Dreams linger, but none shall sleep.

The sun bows low, its light unwinds,
A hush descends, the world aligns.
In twilight's grasp, the secrets fold,
Stories linger, quietly told.

The distant hills, they sigh and breathe,
In every breath, the dusk bequeaths.
A moment caught in tender time,
Where silence sings, and stars will climb.

Through whispers low, the night will reign,
As echoes dance on silver rain.
Where hope is found in fading light,
A journey starts, beneath the night.

Silhouettes Beneath the Veil

Silhouettes in muted hue,
Beneath the veil, the shadows grew.
Softly whispering tales of old,
In forgotten dreams, the hearts unfold.

A lantern's glow, flickers slight,
Guides the way through darkened night.
Each silhouette tells a story,
A dance of life, an ancient glory.

As moonlight spills on fields of gray,
In silence, night finds its way.
Veils of mist drift gently by,
In their embrace, we learn to fly.

Echoes linger in the shade,
Where secrets form and fears evade.
Together we drift, hand in hand,
Beneath the veil, we understand.

Echoes in Gloomy Meadows

In gloomy meadows, shadows cast,
Footsteps whisper of the past.
Echoes wander, lost in time,
Silent stories, a fading rhyme.

The flowers bow, their colors dim,
As twilight sings its solemn hymn.
In the stillness, secrets bloom,
Hearts entwined within the gloom.

A gentle breeze, a rustled sigh,
Softly calls the stars on high.
Each blade of grass a voice to lend,
As echoes weave, the night descends.

Through the haze, a glimmer's found,
In shadows deep, we feel the sound.
Together, lost in timeless flow,
In gloomy meadows, love will grow.

Twilight's Embrace

In twilight's embrace, the day does fade,
Soft colors blend, as dreams invade.
A hush hangs low, a tender sigh,
Where sun and moon begin to try.

The stars awaken, one by one,
To paint the night, a dance begun.
In whispers sweet, the shadows play,
As twilight gently steals the day.

Through the stillness, memories gleam,
Like silver threads in a fragile dream.
We hold the light in gentle grace,
In every moment, twilight's trace.

With hearts alight, we greet the night,
In twilight's arms, everything feels right.
Together we drift, in starlit seams,
Where love is found, and life redeems.

Reflections in the Mist

Gentle whispers drift and sway,
Echoes lost in dawn's soft light.
Mirrored dreams in shades of gray,
Veil the world in serene flight.

Silent waters, deep and clear,
Capture secrets that we seek.
Hidden visions drawing near,
Murmur softly, never speak.

Shadows dance on quiet streams,
Painting tales of days gone by.
In this realm of waking dreams,
Truths arise like misty sighs.

With each breath, the stillness grows,
Nature's hand in tender touch.
Reflections speak where no one goes,
Inviting hearts to feel so much.

Requiem for the Light

In the dusk, the shadows blend,
Fleeting glimmers fade away.
Whispers of the sun descend,
    Softly ushering the gray.

A mournful chime of twilight calls,
Echoes of the day's sweet grace.
As the fiery brilliance falls,
Nighttime dons her velvet lace.

Stars awaken, one by one,
Painting darkness with their glow.
In the silence, dreams are spun,
Of the warmth we used to know.

Let the shadows take their course,
Embrace the night and all it brings.
In the stillness, find remorse,
    Echoing the lost sun's wings.

The Sigh of Forgotten Corners

Dusty books and cobwebbed frames,
Tell the stories left behind.
Faded photographs bear names,
Whispers trapped in ties that bind.

In the corners, shadows creep,
Silent echoes of the past.
Moments captured, secrets keep,
Time slips by, forever fast.

Memories held in quiet halls,
Fragments of a life once bold.
In the stillness, a soft call,
Tales of warmth in whispers told.

As we wander, hearts entwine,
Finding solace in the lost.
Each sigh breathes a tender line,
Reminding us of what it cost.

Hallowed Shades of Dusk

Underneath the twilight's gaze,
Voices stir in soft refrain.
In the beauty of the haze,
Day and night, they waltz again.

Gentle breezes pull and tease,
Nature's hymn, a soothing grace.
Here, the soul finds quiet ease,
In the dusk, a warm embrace.

Golden hues and shadows play,
Painting moments pure and bright.
In the dusk, we pause to stay,
Savoring the blend of light.

Hallowed are these fleeting times,
Here where dreams and peace might blend.
Each heartbeat sings in quiet rhymes,
As the day begins to end.

When Daylight Fades

The sun dips low, the sky turns gray,
Shadows stretch as night claims day.
Stars awaken in silent flight,
Whispers echo in fading light.

The world softens, a gentle sigh,
Colors blend in the twilight sky.
A hush falls over the sleepy lane,
As dreams begin to dance again.

Moonlight spills on the quiet ground,
A soothing peace, a tender sound.
All is wrapped in silken night,
When daylight fades, the heart takes flight.

In this stillness, time stands still,
Beneath the stars, we find our will.
As night enfolds its dark embrace,
We step into a timeless space.

Memories Cast in Shade

In corners dim where echoes dwell,
The past unfolds its ancient spell.
Fleeting moments, captured grace,
Whisper softly, a warm embrace.

Shadows lengthen, secrets turn,
Flickering flames from embers burn.
Thoughts entwine in twilight's glow,
Silent stories begin to flow.

Each memory, a fragile thread,
Woven lightly through the dread.
In the shade, our hearts align,
Finding solace in what's benign.

A tapestry of joy and woe,
In the night, our feelings grow.
Underneath the watchful trees,
We cherish time, our souls at ease.

Constellations of the Dim World

Stars above in scattered lines,
Whisper secrets, ancient signs.
In the dark, they guide our way,
Odd companions of the fray.

Planets shimmer, a distant dance,
In the quiet, we take a chance.
Galaxies swirl, a cosmic tide,
In the vastness, dreams collide.

Journeys stretch through endless night,
Constellations share their light.
Each twinkle tells a tale of old,
In their glow, the brave and bold.

We reach for those celestial flames,
Hoping to forge our own names.
In this tapestry of dark and bright,
We find ourselves in shared flight.

The Unseen's Lament

In shadows deep, where silence weeps,
The unseen sorrow vigil keeps.
A breathless plea, a softened call,
In quiet corners, we feel it all.

Names forgotten, faces blurred,
Whispers linger, barely heard.
They haunt the spaces in between,
The tales of loss, we've never seen.

Yearning hearts in shades of grey,
Long for light, to find their way.
Yet in this gloom, resilience lies,
And bold rebirth beneath the skies.

We mourn the unseen, but we also grow,
Through shadows' veil, a brighter glow.
The lament brings forth a new refrain,
In the stillness, hope remains.

The Essence of Fading Forms

In the garden where flowers once bloomed,
Petals fall like memories consumed.
Soft whispers dance in the late summer air,
Echoes of beauty, lingering rare.

Time weaves shadows on the old stone,
Silently marking what we have known.
A fading picture of days long passed,
In the twilight, these moments last.

Nature's brush strokes in muted hues,
Remind us of laughter and joyful blues.
Yet every form, in time, shall wane,
Leaving traces of love and pain.

So we gather these fragments so dear,
In the heart's cradle, shed no tear.
For in fading forms, light still resides,
Carving paths where the spirit hides.

Shades of Unforgotten Whispers

In the hush of the night, secrets breathe,
Softly woven like a spider's weave.
Faint echoes call from shadows unseen,
Where time forgets the spaces between.

Voices linger in the cool midnight air,
Their stories carved with delicate care.
Each whisper a thread of what once was,
Threaded together without much pause.

The moonlight spills on a tapestry grand,
Guiding lost souls through an unseen hand.
In the stillness, old dreams come to play,
Dancing with ghosts at the end of the day.

In every shadow, a tale yet untold,
Of love, of sorrow, of courage bold.
So we listen, with hearts open wide,
For shades of whispers begin to collide.

Glimmering Shadows of Legacy

Among ancient trees, stories remain,
Tales of valor, loss, and gain.
Roots entwined in the soil of time,
Glimmering shadows, a silent rhyme.

With every leaf that dances and sways,
Echoes of laughter weave through the maze.
In the twilight glow, we see their grace,
In memories held, no need for a place.

Stars overhead bear witness to dreams,
While the river flows with whispered themes.
Legacy shines in the heart's embrace,
Tracing our steps through this sacred space.

In every heartbeat, the past intertwines,
Lessons engraved in the fabric of times.
So let us stand on this storied ground,
With glimmering shadows forever profound.

The Secret Beneath the Dusk

As the sun dips low, the horizon glows,
Secrets awaken where the night wind blows.
Whispers of twilight drift softly near,
Unraveling tales that we long to hear.

Hidden beneath is the softest sigh,
A longing that reaches towards the sky.
In the fading light, dreams softly blend,
With the promise of night, where stories extend.

Stars emerge, like twinkling eyes,
Guardians of secrets that deeply lie.
In the shade of dusk, we find our way,
To the depths of our hearts, where shadows play.

So we gather these moments, gentle and meek,
Unraveling mysteries, in silence we speak.
For beyond the dusk, in the silence we trust,
Lies a world reborn, in the twilight's dust.

Fables from the Gloaming

In twilight's grasp, the shadows weave,
Tales of old, in whispers, cleave.
Creatures dance beneath the trees,
Silent echoes on the breeze.

Stars awaken, lanterns bright,
Guiding dreams through the night.
Fables spun from silver thread,
Where the lost find paths to tread.

Softly spoken, secrets shared,
In the gloaming, none are scared.
Voices call from realms unknown,
In this twilight, we are home.

Beneath the moon's soft embrace,
Every heart finds its place.
Fables whispered, softly sung,
In the gloaming, we are young.

A Ballad to the Unknown

Beyond horizons, shadows play,
A ballad calls for those astray.
In the distance, whispers sway,
Promising the break of day.

Lost in dreams, we search the night,
With every step, we chase the light.
Voices haunt like ghosts of old,
Their stories waiting to be told.

Through the mist where mysteries dwell,
We wander on, under their spell.
Each corner turned, a chance to find,
The truths that linger in the mind.

With open hearts, we face the dawn,
A tapestry of hope is drawn.
In the unknown, we find our song,
A ballad to which we belong.

Journey through the Shimmering Gloom

In twilight's haze, we start to roam,
Through shimmering gloom, we seek a home.
Footsteps soft on hallowed ground,
Echoing dreams, a haunting sound.

Silvery veils of mist enfold,
Each secret glimmering like gold.
Wandering souls in search of grace,
Painted stars in endless space.

With every heartbeat, shadows sway,
Guiding us through night and day.
In the gloom, we find our way,
To the light of a new display.

A journey wrapped in whispered lore,
Unlocking every hidden door.
In shimmering darkness, we aspire,
To dance upon the edge of fire.

Constellations of Dread

In the inky depths of night,
Constellations flicker, faint light.
Each star a story, woven tight,
Of fears that echo, taking flight.

Whispers dark like shadows creep,
In the silence, sorrows steep.
Lost in thoughts, we tremble, dread,
As specters rise from dreams we shed.

Yet in the darkness, hope remains,
A flicker lost in many chains.
For every star that sparks the fear,
There's a memory held so dear.

In the cosmos, we intertwine,
Constellations of dread align.
A tapestry of joy and pain,
In the void, a promise gained.

Embracing the Dimness

In shadows deep where whispers play,
The night unveils its soft decay.
Beneath the veil of twilight's grace,
We find our peace in hidden space.

A gentle hush, a tender sigh,
The stars emerge to light the sky.
In every crack, in every seam,
We traverse paths of quiet dream.

Undercurrents of the Evening

The sun dips low, the sky's aglow,
With secrets wrapped where breezes flow.
Beneath the branches, shadows creep,
An echo stirs from twilight's sleep.

Soft murmurs rise from starlit streams,
In the stillness, hope redeems.
Each fleeting breath a whispered tune,
Awakens hearts beneath the moon.

Trails of the Phantom Light

A flicker dances, ghostly bright,
In corridors of fading light.
We tread on paths where phantoms weave,
Their stories linger, hearts believe.

Amidst the shadows, truth takes flight,
With every step, we chase the night.
Through veiled illusions, we will roam,
In search of whispers leading home.

Chasing Twilight Dreams

The day surrenders to night's embrace,
As dreams cascade in gentle grace.
Each moment drips with golden hue,
Awakening wishes wrapped in blue.

We chase the edges where colors blend,
In twilight's hold, our spirits mend.
With every heartbeat, shadows play,
As night unfolds and steals the day.

Beneath the Veil of Night

Stars whisper softly in the dark,
A silver glow ignites a spark.
Shadows dance with gentle grace,
While dreams unfold in this serene space.

The moon casts light on silent trees,
With every rustle, the heart feels ease.
Night embraces, holding tight,
Wrapped in stillness, pure delight.

Each moment breathes a magic rare,
In this realm without a care.
Secrets linger within the air,
Beneath the veil, the world laid bare.

In twilight's hush, we find our truth,
A journey touched by love and youth.
Here lies the heart's deep, hidden plight,
Forever bound beneath the night.

Secrets of the Gloom

In the depths where shadows dwell,
Whispers echo, casting spell.
Forgotten paths, the unknown leads,
In silence, sown are hidden seeds.

Beneath the figure of despair,
Lies a hope found nowhere rare.
Each sigh, a secret to unbind,
In gloomy depths, a light to find.

Veils of darkness, thick and steep,
Guard the treasures that we keep.
In every fear, a story blooms,
Revealing truths behind the glooms.

Through the mist, a flicker's flair,
Sensitivity fills the air.
In secrets held from sight so soon,
Awaits the dawn, a brightened tune.

Realm of Half-Lights

Between the dusk and breaking dawn,
A world of dreams quietly spawned.
Fading edges blur and swirl,
As mysteries in shadows twirl.

Half-lights dance on tender streams,
Where reality merges with dreams.
Glimmers guide the wandering soul,
In this space, we feel made whole.

The gentle hush of twilight sings,
Secrets carried on whispered wings.
In this realm, we softly tread,
Where hopes are born and fears are shed.

Each heartbeat syncs with the night,
In the glow that feels just right.
Embrace the magic, lost in flight,
In the realm where all is light.

Murmurs from the Abyss

In the depths of silence, echoes call,
Ancient whispers, a soft enthrall.
Voices rise from shadows vast,
Secrets from the present past.

The abyss holds stories untold,
Of dreams once lost and souls so bold.
In its embrace, we dare to think,
As thoughts plunge deep, we start to sink.

Murmurs swirl like evening mist,
A haunting touch, a gentle tryst.
With every ripple, we are drawn,
To the depths where fears are dawned.

In darkness thick, the heart beats clear,
For even voids can breed the near.
From the abyss, a truth prevails,
In every silence, life unveils.

The Dance of Dimming Light

The sun dips low, shadows entwined,
Whispers of dusk, a dance unconfined.
Colors fade in the velvet night,
Stars awaken, ready for flight.

Moonlight glimmers on silent streams,
Fading echoes of forgotten dreams.
Every flicker a gentle sigh,
In the twilight, time slips by.

Branches sway, a soft embrace,
Nature's breath in the quiet space.
As darkness falls, a calm descends,
The day concludes, but never ends.

In this ballet, shadows play,
A fleeting moment before the gray.
Hold onto light, let it ignite,
In the dance of dimming light.

Masquerade of the Unmanifested

Beneath the veil of the unseen,
A spectral glow, a world serene.
Whispers flicker, thoughts collide,
In the masquerade, shadows bide.

Masks of dreams drift in the haze,
Unravel truths in twilight's maze.
Every glance a fleeting spark,
Illusions weave through the dark.

Fingers trace the paths of fate,
Echoed laughter resonates.
In this dance of hidden sights,
We find ourselves in the depths of night.

A symphony of silence calls,
Through the shrouded, shadowed walls.
Join the waltz, embrace the night,
In the masquerade of unmanifested light.

Where Echoes Find Solace

In valleys low, where whispers dwell,
Voices linger, tales to tell.
Every echo finds its place,
In the gentle arms of grace.

Mountains stand like ancient guards,
Holding secrets, keeping shards.
Time flows softly, calm and slow,
Where echoes dance, and memories grow.

Starlit skies watch over head,
Guiding wanderers, gently led.
In this realm of soft embrace,
Every heartbeat finds its space.

The world outside may storm and cry,
But here, in silence, dreams do fly.
Where echoes whisper soft and free,
Solace waits for you and me.

A Chorus of Lost Spirits

In the moonlit glade, voices rise,
A chorus sings beneath dark skies.
Whispers of souls that time forgot,
Bound by chains in a silent plot.

They wade through shadows, soft and light,
Searching for solace in the night.
Every note a tale of woe,
In haunting melodies that flow.

Eyes of ash and hearts of flame,
In the stillness, they call your name.
Echoes of laughter, tears of pain,
A dance of memory in the rain.

Take a step into their song,
Feel their presence, where you belong.
In the chorus of lost spirits bright,
Find the clarity in the night.

Grim Waltz of Shadows

In the twilight's fading glow,
The shadows dance, slow and low.
Whispers thread through the night air,
Calling out, a silent dare.

Figures linger, lost in time,
Echoes weave a haunting rhyme.
With every step, a secret blends,
In the dark, where night extends.

Cold fingers brush the mind's eye,
Fleeting shapes that drift and sigh.
They twirl beneath a silvered moon,
Charting paths that end too soon.

The dance goes on, a shrouded fate,
Where shadows twine, and hearts await.
In their midst, we find our fears,
As shadows waltz amidst our tears.

Mists of Whispers and Woe

Beneath a veil of endless gray,
Whispers dance in frail dismay.
Fingers reach through hazy dreams,
Searching for the light that gleams.

Mist envelops, thick and dense,
Shrouding truths with vague suspense.
Voices call from far and wide,
Echoing the things we hide.

In the gloom, old sorrows wake,
Filling hearts with every ache.
Lost in tales of what has been,
In the mists, we swim unseen.

Yet hope glimmers, faint yet clear,
Carried soft on whispered cheer.
Through the fog, a pathway waits,
Leading forth to open gates.

Beneath the Haze of Day

In the shimmer of the sun's embrace,
Lies a story, lost in space.
Beams of light cast fleeting dreams,
Filling voids with soft moonbeams.

Reality blurs, lines recede,
In this haze, the heart takes heed.
Burdened breaths amid the bright,
Chasing shadows in the light.

Underneath the day's bright gaze,
Linger thoughts in misty haze.
Moments caught like rising smoke,
Words unspoken, silently spoke.

Yet in that soft, elusive glow,
Lies a depth we long to know.
For beneath the haze of light,
Awaits the beauty of the night.

The Lure of Darkened Dreams

In the silence of the night,
Lies a realm, devoid of light.
Dreams entwine in shadowed grace,
Whispers echo, a haunting trace.

Things unseen, they pull us near,
Tales of loss, tales of fear.
In their grip, we float and swirl,
Captured in the darkened whirl.

Fingers grasp at phantom threads,
Drawing closer to what dreads.
Yet within this twisted scheme,
Lies the heart of every dream.

For behind the veil of night,
Is a spark, a hidden light.
The lure of dreams, both dark and bright,
Calls the soul to take its flight.

Dance of the Forgotten

In shadows deep where whispers play,
The forgotten souls begin to sway.
They twirl and spin in a ghostly light,
Caught in the dance of endless night.

Their laughter echoes like fading chimes,
In the sepulchral hush of forgotten times.
With every step, they reclaim a piece,
Of dreams lost in an eternal cease.

The stars above watch from their throne,
As echoes of memories weave and moan.
In this spectral realm, they find their grace,
A dance of the lost in a timeless space.

Beneath the moon's gentle gleam,
They weave through the fabric of forgotten dreams.
In silence, they find what's been long forgot,
An ancient ballet in a desolate spot.

Flickers of the Forgotten Night

In the velvety cloak of dusk's embrace,
Flickers of memory begin to trace.
Flames that once danced now softly sigh,
Whispers of shadows that drift and fly.

Stars blink slowly, like distant tears,
Carrying secrets of forgotten years.
Each twinkle is a fragment of light,
Lost in the depth of a haunting night.

The cool wind carries a long-lost tune,
Beneath the watch of a ghostly moon.
Softly it weaves through the hollow trees,
A melody brushed by the night's soft breeze.

In the silence, the past calls out,
Flickers of life amidst shadows shout.
Embers of love that once brightly burned,
Now flicker and fade, yet we still yearn.

Silhouettes in Silence

Silhouettes blend in the fading light,
Figures once vibrant now hidden from sight.
Echoes of laughter, a distant chime,
Fading like whispers lost in time.

Each shadow a story, each line a tear,
Carved into memories we hold dear.
In this quiet realm where silence reigns,
The heartache lingers, but hope remains.

Under the stars, we search for a sign,
In shadows of silence, our souls entwine.
For in each dark corner, a flicker might glow,
A promise of light when we've lost all hope.

So we dance with the silence, in shadows we tread,
Embracing the tales that the darkness has bred.
In silhouettes whispering of moments past,
We find our solace, we hold it fast.

Enigmas Among the Dark

Among the dark where secrets lie,
Enigmas whisper and shadows sigh.
Each corner turned, a riddle unfolds,
Stories of courage, love, and bold.

The night conceals what daylight dares,
Mysteries draped in the moonlight's cares.
Figures dance with a hidden grace,
Carved from the silence, lost in space.

In echoes soft, the past draws near,
Wrapped in the fog, it lingers here.
With every breath, we feel the pull,
Of enigmas lurking, dark and full.

We listen closely, for fears abide,
In shadows that creep where dreams confide.
Among the dark, may we find our way,
Through enigmas that lead us, night to day.

The Realm Beyond the Veil

In whispers soft, the shadows dance,
Through twilight's grasp, we take a chance.
Beyond the veil, where secrets bide,
In the unknown, we seek to glide.

The stars awaken, eyes so bright,
Leading us through the endless night.
With every breath, a story spun,
In realms where dream and life are one.

The echoes call from distant shores,
Awakening the ancient lore.
In the realm where silence speaks,
The truth is found in wild mystiques.

So venture forth, let spirit sail,
Into the depths of the hidden trail.
Unravel the threads of fate's design,
In the realm where souls entwine.

Crossing the Dim Horizon

A horizon dim, where shadows meet,
The path unfolds beneath our feet.
With every step, the light will fade,
As dreams and fears begin to wade.

The past a whisper, the future unknown,
In twilight's grasp, we wander alone.
Yet in the dark, a spark ignites,
Leading us through the restless nights.

Together we walk, hand in hand,
In the silence, we understand.
The journey holds both pain and grace,
In the dim horizon, we find our place.

So take a breath, let spirits soar,
For on this path, we will explore.
Across the dim horizon wide,
Our hearts will light the endless tide.

Dreams in the Twilight

As daylight fades, dreams softly bloom,
In twilight hues, dispelling gloom.
The stars awaken, shining bright,
Guiding souls through the velvet night.

In every sigh, a wish is sewn,
With whispers sweet, the night is grown.
Beneath a sky of shimmering hues,
New tales emerge, new paths to choose.

Moments linger, suspended in air,
In dreams we dance, free from despair.
The twilight's grace, a gentle balm,
Embracing hearts with a soothing calm.

So close your eyes, let dreams take flight,
In the twilight's arms, feel the delight.
For in this space where shadows play,
Our dreams will shine, come what may.

Guardians of the Obsidian Path

Mysterious lights guide the way,
As we tread the obsidian bay.
Guardians watch with eyes of fire,
Protecting us as we aspire.

In shadows deep, the truth resides,
With ancient whispers, the heart confides.
Each step we take, the echoes sing,
Of champions bold and the tales they bring.

Together we stand on this sacred ground,
In unity's strength, our purpose found.
Through trials faced and darkness known,
In the obsidian path, we've truly grown.

So harness light, let courage reign,
For in our hearts, we break the chain.
Guardians strong, with spirits vast,
On the obsidian path, we hold steadfast.

Beneath Starlit Obscurities

In the hush of night, we wander wide,
Dreams take flight where secrets hide.
Silent whispers through the trees,
Carried softly by the breeze.

Stars above like scattered dreams,
Guiding us with silver beams.
Each step led by moon's soft glow,
Into the depths of night we go.

Shadows dance on pathways lost,
Embers fade but never exhaust.
Through the dark, a tale unfolds,
Of muted heartbeats, brave and bold.

As dawn peeks through, we'll still remain,
Chasing echoes, knowing their name.
For beneath starlit obscurities,
Our spirits soar, our hearts at ease.

Journeys through the Umbral Realm

In twilight's grip, adventures call,
Through veils of night, the shadows fall.
With lanterns lit, we seek the way,
Through corridors of lost decay.

Veils of mist, so softly spun,
Bringing forth what's left undone.
Each path a tale, each turn a sign,
Guided by stars that intertwine.

Whispers echo through the trees,
Carried softly on the breeze.
In this realm where secrets dwell,
Every journey holds a spell.

So let us tread on unseen ground,
Where mysteries and freedom are found.
Together through the umbral light,
Chasing dreams into the night.

Shadows of Unseen Paths

In the depths where whispers rise,
Shadows linger, hidden lies.
Through the thicket, branches sway,
Leading us along the fray.

Footsteps soft on ancient stone,
Echoes of the past well known.
In the twilight's warm embrace,
We discover our heart's place.

Vague horizons call us near,
Filling souls with hope and fear.
Through the dark, we glean the truth,
Nurtured dreams of timeless youth.

Yet as we wander, hand in hand,
Shadows weave a hidden strand.
Treading forth on unseen paths,
Finding light through gentle wrath.

The Realm of Fading Echoes

In the quiet where whispers fade,
Echoes linger, memories laid.
Every heartbeat marks the time,
Lost in rhythm, soft as chime.

Through the halls where silence reigns,
Fading laughter, soft refrains.
In this realm of ghostly dreams,
Life is not what it seems.

Wandering through the veils of past,
Each moment's shadow, fleeting cast.
Holding onto threads of light,
In the dark, we find our sight.

So let the echoes guide our ways,
Through the haze of endless days.
In the realm where memories dance,
We embrace the fleeting chance.

Tapestry of Shadows

Whispers weave through the night air,
Fingers trace secrets unseen.
Shadows dance in moonlit glare,
A silent song, serene.

Threads of darkness intertwine,
Stories lost in twilight's hush.
Every corner starts to shine,
In the quiet, hearts rush.

Reflections born from fear's embrace,
Fraying edges of the light.
In this place, we find our space,
Navigating through the night.

Beneath this veil, we hold our breath,
Memories linger like smoke.
In every shadow, life and death,
In every silence, words evoke.

The Space Between Day and Night

Where dusk meets dawn in gentle sighs,
A canvas painted in gray hues.
The world suspended, time defies,
In this stillness, thoughts diffuse.

Stars peek gently, shy and bright,
Echoing dreams that softly call.
Fleeting moments twist in flight,
As shadows start to rise and fall.

Colors blend in whispered tones,
The sun and moon engage their dance.
In this realm, where warmth condones,
All of life holds its expanse.

Here within this twilight hour,
Hope ignites in fading light.
And every heartbeat holds its power,
In that space between day and night.

Hues of Uncertainty

Brushstrokes falter on the page,
Shades of doubt linger near.
Life's too vivid, yet we gauge,
What we lose and what we fear.

Colors clash, a vivid fight,
In the chaos, truth may hide.
Every mix brings new insight,
In the tumult, hearts take stride.

Moments flicker, fleeting chance,
Caught in life's unpredictable blend.
Each mistake holds its own dance,
A spectrum, as we transcend.

Though the path may seem unclear,
In the waves of joy and grief,
Every hue we hold so dear,
Paints the canvas of belief.

The Wane of Visibility

Glimmers fade as twilight looms,
Shapes dissolve, shadows creep.
In the silence, dark consumes,
Leaving whispers in its sweep.

Lights flicker, once so bright,
Now retreating from the fray.
As the stars begin their flight,
We find solace in the gray.

Faint impressions trace our fears,
Echoes dance in fading light.
Through the darkness, hope appears,
Guiding us beyond the night.

In the gloom, we seek the dawn,
With each heartbeat, dreams revive.
As the veil of night is drawn,
We awaken, we survive.

The Gentle Pull of Dusk

The sun sinks low, a tender gaze,
Painting skies in blush and haze.
Whispers float on evening's breath,
As day surrenders, dancing with death.

A hush descends, the world grows still,
Night's velvet cloak begins to fill.
Stars emerge, like secrets shared,
In twilight's embrace, we find we cared.

The edges blur, where light meets dark,
Crickets sing their nightly spark.
Gentle shadows start to creep,
In this magic, we softly leap.

With each soft step, the night unfolds,
In whispered tales, the heart beholds.
The gentle pull, a soothing hymn,
As dusk leads us to dreams within.

Shadows on the Fringe

In corners deep where silence hides,
Shadows linger, truth abides.
Echoes whisper from the past,
Through fleeting glances, memories cast.

Figures dance just out of sight,
A haunting pulse in fading light.
Beneath the weight of ancient trees,
The secrets linger on the breeze.

Lost in thought, our minds do roam,
In this twilight, we find a home.
Each shadow hides a story told,
In muted tones, both brave and bold.

They beckon softly to draw us near,
A touch of comfort, a hint of fear.
In the quiet, we learn to trust,
The shadows on the fringe of dust.

The Forgotten Echo Chamber

A room of echoes, frail and worn,
Where laughter fades, and hopes are torn.
Walls adorned with whispers faint,
Memories tangled, lost in paint.

Footsteps linger, dust motes dance,
Each creak and sigh, a fleeting chance.
Ghosts of dreams that never soared,
In this chamber, our hearts are stored.

Time stands still, a frozen race,
In shadows cast, we meet our grace.
Words unspoken float in air,
In this chamber, silence dares.

A sanctuary of what could be,
The forgotten holds a key to see.
In the stillness, truth reclaimed,
The echo chamber, never tamed.

Lurkers of the Twilit Path

Upon the trail where shadows play,
Lurkers hide, both night and day.
Their whispers weave through autumn leaves,
An ancient dance, each heart perceives.

Beneath the boughs, mysteries breathe,
Hidden wonders in the sleeve.
The twilight hums with stories old,
Of spirits wandering, brave and bold.

Eyes in the dark, they softly gleam,
Guardians of each fleeting dream.
In shrouded woods where secrets dwell,
Lurkers weave their timeless spell.

As footsteps stumble, they appear,
In the quiet, we sense their near.
With every twist of nature's thread,
The path unravels where hopes are led.

Threads of Illusive Dawn

Soft whispers weave through skies anew,
Golden hues replace the starry dew.
Waking dreams in the morning light,
Gentle hands pull away the night.

Each fiber spun with hope's embrace,
Fading shadows, they leave no trace.
As daybreak breathes on timid stone,
The world stirs softly, not alone.

In this dance of light and shade,
A tapestry of moments laid.
Imagined paths, where visions blend,
Dawn's first kiss, it will not end.

With every thread that we discern,
In shadows past, we start to learn.
From quietude the day takes flight,
Threads of dusk bring morning's light.

When Night Holds Its Breath

The world falls silent, stars align,
In stillness, secrets intertwine.
Moonlit shadows waltz on the ground,
Echoes of dreams, they swirl around.

Time seems to pause in this deep sigh,
As whispers of wishes drift up high.
Crickets play a soft serenade,
While the earth beneath is gently laid.

Every heartbeat echoes in the dark,
Lit only by the fireflies' spark.
When night holds its breath, we all wait,
To glimpse the magic that it creates.

In the hush of night, we become whole,
Finding solace deep in our soul.
For when darkness breathes its last tune,
It gives way to the light of the moon.

Grasping at Ethereal Silhouettes

Fleeting figures drift in the air,
Whispers of dreams, stroking my hair.
Shadows dance on the edges of thought,
Grasping at wonders, never caught.

A twilight haze veils the wandering,
Where memories linger, softly plundering.
Each glance a flicker of what could be,
Ethereal echoes, wild and free.

In twilight's embrace, I find my way,
To fleeting moments that softly sway.
Fingers reach out to seize the light,
But dissolve like mist, lost from sight.

Chasing phantoms, I wander alone,
Through whispered secrets, I find my home.
As stars ignite in a velvet sea,
Grasping at silhouettes, I find me.

Silence Beneath a Shroud

A cloak of quiet wraps the night,
Stars blink softly, veiled in white.
Beneath the shroud, the world lies still,
Waiting for time to bend at will.

Soft breath of winds, a muted song,
Where shadows play, we all belong.
In gentle moments, the heart can weave,
A tapestry of hope, believe.

With every hush, a story's told,
In silence deep, the dreams unfold.
Secrets held in the dark embrace,
Where silence dances, a timeless grace.

As dawn approaches with a sigh,
The quiet bids a soft goodbye.
In the shroud of night, we find our breath,
In silence born, we learn of depth.

Playgrounds of the Enigmatic Night

Underneath the starlit sky,
Children's laughter fades on by.
Mystery lingers in the breeze,
Whispers dance among the trees.

Shadows stretch with dreams in hand,
Secrets spun in silver sand.
The moonlight plays, a gentle guide,
In this realm where dreams reside.

Footprints lost in cosmic flight,
Tales are spun in cloaks of night.
Echoes of the unseen past,
In this playground, shadows cast.

Silent songs of ages old,
Stories waiting to be told.
In the stillness, hearts ignite,
In the playground of the night.

Echoes in the Forgotten Realm

In the valley lost to time,
Whispers weave a subtle rhyme.
Ancient stones recall the lore,
Ghostly voices at the door.

Beneath the foliage, secrets lie,
Echoes of a long-lost cry.
Footsteps linger in the mist,
In shadows where dreams coexist.

Time stands still in twilight's grasp,
Memories in silence clasp.
Winds of change, they softly call,
In the realm forgotten by all.

Fables written in the air,
Linger here, a timeless prayer.
In the echoes, hearts can feel,
The pulse of a forgotten reel.

Whispers in Twilight

Dusk descends with a gentle sigh,
As day bids the world goodbye.
Colors blend in soft embrace,
In twilight's warm and tender space.

Silent whispers haunt the air,
Secrets spoken with great care.
Stars begin their nightly play,
In the twilight, night holds sway.

Cooler breezes start to sing,
To the magic night can bring.
Footprints fall on ancient ground,
In whispers where lost dreams are found.

Moonlight casts a silver sheen,
In the calm, a soft serene.
Hearts awaken to the light,
In the whispers of the night.

Echoes of Dusk

As the sun slips from the day,
Colors fade and shadows play.
In the hush of evening's glow,
Whispers dance, they come and go.

Fading light, a solemn tone,
Echoes of the day now flown.
All the dreams that paint the sky,
Sift through fingers, softly sigh.

Memories drift like fallen leaves,
In the dusk, the spirit weaves.
Tales of yore, a nightingale,
Sings of paths where hearts can sail.

In this hour before the night,
A silent world begins to write.
Echoes linger, gently sweet,
In the dusk, our souls will meet.

Sable Whispers of the Heart

In the shadowed corners, secrets dwell,
Softly they echo, a whispered spell.
Memories flutter like leaves in the breeze,
Carried on night air, with haunting ease.

Silken threads weave through the silence profound,
Echoes of love in the darkness are found.
Fleeting yet faithful, like stars that ignite,
Glimmering softly, fading from sight.

Hearts intertwined in a dance of despair,
Yearning for warmth in a world cold and bare.
Sable whispers linger, a bittersweet sigh,
A tapestry woven of love's gentle cry.

Yet even in shadows, hope starts to bloom,
In the depths of sorrow, dispelling the gloom.
Embers of passion still flicker and call,
Lifting the veil, love conquers it all.

Labyrinth of Faded Promises

In the maze of whispers, promises fade,
Echoing dreams in the twilight shade.
Paths intertwining, lost in their twists,
Memory's ghosts in the air still persist.

Worn maps of longing sketch out the way,
Tracing the footsteps of yesterday.
Promises linger where silence resides,
In the heart of the labyrinth, truth abides.

But shadows creep in with their silent refrain,
Doubts like thorns pierce a heart full of pain.
Yet somewhere within this intricate maze,
Hope flickers on in a delicate blaze.

Every turn leads to a secret untold,
Stories of warmth wrapped in ice-cold mold.
Yet through the darkness, a light soon will shine,
Revealing the beauty of love's grand design.

Cradle of Lingering Sorrows

In the cradle of shadows, sorrow takes flight,
Cradled softly in the stillness of night.
Whispers of heartache dance on the air,
Lingering echoes of love's cruel dare.

Empty embraces haunt every sigh,
Fading shadows where the memories lie.
Cradled in longing, the heart beats alone,
Gathering fragments of dreams overthrown.

Time weaves its tapestry, delicate threads,
Stitching the past where the heart never treads.
Yet amidst the sorrow, a glimmer may show,
Healing in whispers, soft as the snow.

Cradle the ache, let it meld with the soul,
For every sorrow plays its vital role.
In the dance of existence, life ebbs and flows,
Even in darkness, resilience still grows.

Soliloquies in the Half-Light

In the half-light's glow, stories unwind,
Each voice a soft echo of what we don't find.
Soliloquies rise like mist from the ground,
In whispers of longing, lost loves abound.

Shadows entwine as the day starts to fade,
Emotions painted in hues, unafraid.
Words linger softly like dew on the grass,
Filling the silence with moments that pass.

Caught in a reverie, eyes searching the dark,
The heart speaks in verses, igniting a spark.
Through the silence, a melody flows,
In the half-light's embrace, the essence bestows.

No more a mere echo, no longer confined,
Expressions of longing, beautifully aligned.
In the realm of twilight, truth finds its way,
Soliloquies blossom, come what may.

Flickers of the Lost

In the twilight's gentle sigh,
Memories drift like fireflies,
Whispered tales of days gone by,
Fleeting, like a soft goodbye.

Silhouettes dance on the wall,
Echoes of a distant call,
Promises that rise and fall,
In the shadows, we stand tall.

Time slips through our grasping hands,
Like tides that shape the shifting sands,
Each flicker of the lost expands,
A tapestry that life demands.

In the silence, we find peace,
From the past, we seek release,
Flickers fade but never cease,
In our hearts, they find their lease.

Between the Veils of Night

Stars emerge in the dark sky,
Whispers carried by the breeze,
Dreams awaken, daring to fly,
Caught between the rustling trees.

Moonlight bathes the world in grace,
Casting shadows, soft and light,
In this stillness, we find our place,
Between the veils of tender night.

Moments linger in the hush,
Time slows down in this embrace,
Every heartbeat, every rush,
Held within the night's warm space.

As dawn approaches, dreams will sway,
Fleeting visions, drift away,
Yet forever, in shadows play,
Between the veils, we'll find our way.

Shadows of Silent Echoes

In the corners of our minds,
Shadows whisper tales unspoken,
Silent echoes, love that binds,
Fragmented words, promises broken.

Memories linger like the haze,
Fading light at the end of day,
In this maze of time's cruel play,
Shadows guide us, lead the way.

Beneath the weight of what we lose,
We find the strength to carry on,
In the silent echoes, we choose,
To mend our hearts by dawn's sweet song.

Though darkness falls, we'll find the light,
In each shadow, hope ignites,
Whispers of the day in flight,
Shadows dance in starry nights.

Shrouded in Nostalgia

In the attic of the heart,
Memories dusted, worn with care,
Fragments of a world apart,
Shrouded in a timeless air.

Photographs of laughter's glow,
Moments freeze in frames of gold,
Time whispers tales of long ago,
Secrets that the silence holds.

Every scent a door unlocked,
Echoes of a life once lived,
In the stories softly rocked,
Nostalgia is the gift we give.

Though the years may drift away,
In our minds, they ever stay,
Shrouded in nostalgia's sway,
A comfort found in yesterday.